ANCHOR BOOKS

EXPRESSIONS

Edited by

Claire Tupholme

First published in Great Britain in 2002 by
ANCHOR BOOKS
Remus House,
Coltsfoot Drive,
Peterborough, PE2 9JX
Telephone (01733) 898102

HB ISBN 1 85930 954 2
SB ISBN 1 85930 959 3

FOREWORD

Anchor Books is a small press, established in 1992, with the aim of promoting readable poetry to as wide an audience as possible.

We hope to establish an outlet for writers of poetry who may have struggled to see their work in print.

The poems presented here have been selected from many entries. Editing proved to be a difficult task and as the Editor, the final selection was mine.

I trust this selection will delight and please the authors and all those who enjoy reading poetry.

Claire Tupholme
Editor

Knowing   (HAIKU)
on page 120.
Written by
    Susan Carole Roberts

CONTENTS

REMEMBER

Remember? Do I remember my first love so well.
Oh how could I truly not remember?
Head over heels in love we fell.

We were merely six yet we could tell
The first time we met in school in September.
Remember? Do I remember my first love well.

She was sobbing as we met before the school bell,
Being pulled by her mother, the girl was so slender.
Head over heels in love we fell.

Sharing swings and water from the pump at the well,
We sang Elvis' 'Love Me Tender'.
Remember? I do remember my first love well.

We were good for each other, coming out of our shell,
Then, she was gone or moved by the following December.
Head over heels in love we fell.

Where did she go? I wanted to yell!
She'd no memories of me fifteen years later.
Remember? I do remember my first love well,
Head over heels in love we fell.

Lloyd Noyes

THE MARRIAGE VOWS

The marriage vows you take this day
That make you man and wife
Will start you on a journey
That carries on through life

May all the dreams you dream today
In coming years unfold
And give you treasured memories
That you alone can hold

The trials and tribulations
A married life can bring
Will let you know there's more to it
Than a licence and a ring

But with love and understanding
You'll find a common ground
It's through a true commitment
That happiness is found

A lifetime is for learning
So take a little time
To learn the art of sharing
And make it yours and mine

You may never own a palace
Or lay claim to any throne
But the secret is in learning
How to make a house your home

Make time for one another
And never be too proud
If you need to say you're sorry
Then say it right out loud

Don't take it all for granted
And don't forget to say
How much you love each other
And mention it each day

May your lives be filled with laughter
That leaves no room for tears
May I wish you health and happiness
And good luck for future years

Christine Lannen

BUTTERFLY

I am a little caterpillar and cabbage I love to eat
I can move fast in the garden, as I have many feet
Some people like to hold me as I wiggle on my way
But I prefer to be alone and eat greens every day
For soon I will be sleeping, in a warm cocoon
Waiting for the right time, when out of there I'll zoom
I will fly up to the sunshine, with lovely coloured wings
For then I'll be a butterfly, one of creation's beautiful things.

M E Smith

SOOTHSAYER

Soothsayer! Soothsayer!
Won't you answer my prayer,
Will my children be dark or fair,
Will they have blonde or auburn hair,
Will you study my stars,
To see if I have a dignified Mars,
Will my life be free from danger,
Will I meet a handsome stranger,
Can you see what will the future hold,
Please tell me what is foretold,
Will I wear a band of gold,
Can you cast the runes for me,
Or read the tea leaves from the tea
What will my planetary positions be,
Will I earn a lot of money,
Will all my days be trouble-free and sunny,

You have Scorpio on the cusp my dear,
And your days will be free from fear,
A better time is drawing near,
Your heart line
Shows that you wait and pine,
An Aries man will be thine,
As to what the stars have in store,
They have for you surprises galore,
You will travel and more besides,
Look through a green door and see what hides,
You will never have to count the stitches,
The path ahead is paved with riches,
But beware,
Of a woman with ginger hair,
That is all I can tell ye!
You see the future lies in your hands.
God only knows and understands.

Alan Pow

DOWN RIVER

River circles come and go
Drifting waters gently flow,
Around the rocks and down wind blow,
Through the valley lands below.

David Bilsborrow

I REMEMBER IT WELL

I remember in my younger years
That Mum and Dad would calm my fears.
And then there came my schoolboy days,
Of school and mates I have every praise.
Progressing on towards my teens
I found a job to eke out my means.
At length through Britain's darkest hour
Our good old Winnie came to power.

I remember towards my middle life
I met a dream girl who became my wife.
Her grace and charm tore my heart asunder;
How I loved my sweetheart from 'Down Under'.
We raised two children – a girl and boy,
Indeed they are our pride and joy.
Now married with children of their own
We delight in seeing them at our home.

I remember the day when I had to retire
With time to live as we desire.
To visit places overseas
And live a life of moderate ease.
To walk the dog around the park
And let him run and play and bark;
To tend the garden – run the car
But nowadays it is not far.

I remember the good things of my life
Especially my children and loving wife.
For now my life is nearly done,
I have my memories – I've had my fun.
And when I leave this earthly sphere
To depart from those I hold most dear,
I only hope that there may be
Some folk behind who will remember me.

Douglas Wood

WHEN I DIE

Bury me not in a cemetery
When I am dead and gone
But throw my ashes to the wind
And let me travel on.

Bury me not in a wooden box
Imprisoned in the ground
But scatter me on open plains
Where freedom can be found.

Bury me not on hallowed land
Don't let me die in vain
Release me from my earthen bonds
And set me free again.

Scatter me not where others lie
Despatch me on my own
Don't let me blow among the dead
Where graves are overgrown.

Scatter me from the highest point
Or throw me into the sea
Or shake me into daffodils
But let my soul be free.

Linda Cooper

A HOLIDAY

Today the sky is ever so light blue,
Little puffs of cloud do meander through,
It's a day for lazing about, all right,
Just simply waiting for the moon at night.

The air is still, nothing stirs, it's too hot,
Even by the pool, movement – there is not a jot,
The only noise to be heard is the ice cream chimes,
Tempting the sun worshippers from their 'Times'.

The boats are coming in with fishing catch,
Men must prepare them for a quick despatch,
To the fishmongers at their shops and stalls,
Whereupon buyers demolish the hauls.

Soon the beach becomes less populated,
Pangs of hunger overtake in masses the sun sated,
The temptation to eat is much too great to be denied,
So to go back to hotels and homes they have tried.

After a freshen up and being refuelled, came back to life,
Time now to hit the hot spots with the wife,
Drink and dance and drink some more,
Party places to go to in galore,
Time now to return, before losing track,
Where did time go to? You can't get it back.

Days have drifted into nights and nights into days,
Resting on the beach to catch the sun's rays,
Alas! The last day is nigh, tomorrow we go,
Leaving behind a part of us, you know.

Mary Lawson

THE MISTRESS

Into the boat he steps, sits gently down;
Eases her back and sees the moorings' rift;
The calls and clamour of the market town
Grow distant as they catch the river's drift.

Soft autumn sunlight warm upon his back;
Still water mirrors sky and trees ahead;
The oars skim smoothly through the river's wrack
And cares slip from him and his duties shed.

The anxious lines etched on his face dispel;
His wary eyes grow softer with the view;
The magic of the water weaves its spell
To rest his body and his soul renew.

As sunset colours paint the evening red,
He steers the vessel on her homeward way;
He leaves his mistress to her lonely bed;
Armed with the strength to face another day.

Dee Yates

A LONELY WORLD

In lonely house, on lonely street.
Lonely man, no one to greet.
Sitting there, in lonely chair.
Waiting to climb, lonely stair.
To rest his head, on lonely bed.
By lonely tears, lonely shed.
In lonely sleep, till lonely dawn.
Who brings with her, a lonely morn.
To a lonely house, on lonely street.
Lonely man, no one to greet.

Jim Cuthbert

OUR WEDDING DAY

Way back in 1953
On our special wedding day,
When we woke up in the morning,
The sky looked cold and grey.

The fog was hanging low
Over the countryside,
But how I prayed the sun would shine,
On my groom, and me the happy bride.

But as the morning passed us by,
The fog slowly faded away,
And the sun came peeping through,
To give us a perfect day.

Although it is forty-eight years ago,
We still remember it well,
How the sun came out and blessed our day,
What a wonderful story to tell.

Iris Covell

PARTY TIME

Mustard, custard, thick and yellow,
Boil it up then add some Jello,
Pour it in a rabbit mould,
Pop in the fridge until set cold.

Take the spoon and dish it out,
To all the kids who did shout,
'Me please, me please! - Well, here it comes,
On every plate for expectant tums.

I watch their faces light up with glee,
So glad they've come to my birthday tea,
They dip their spoons then raise to lips,
The mustard, custard with Jello bits.

And in it goes with sheer delight,
And my eyes dart around taking in the sight,
Oh! Wonder of wonders, all the bulging eyes,
I tell you folks, I deserved a prize.

Then - out it came, in torrents from all,
And thus it started my rapid downfall,
For it splattered my body and was gooey and thick,
And the joke backfired, 'cos it was me that was sick!

Diane Stowell

THE SEVENTH AGE

When you cease to be sprightly
And may suffer pain nightly,
When you're thwarted by tightly
Closed bottles, packets and jars . . .

When you've given up hoarding
And find it most rewarding
To have kind help when boarding
Buses, taxis, trains and cars . . .

When words get harder hearing
And you feel you are nearing
The time when you'll be peering
Through very much stronger specs . . .

When you seem more forgetful
And a little regretful
Of chances missed, and fretful
Of imagined slights and checks . . .

When policemen *are* younger
And you no longer hunger
For gossip, which its monger
May spread with gloom and alarm . . .

Then you've reached a certain age
When you've read most every page
Of Book of Life, entering stage
Of well-deserved rest and calm!

Geoffrey Matthews

MINIATURE SYMPHONY

Beneath a weeping willow
Branches dipping in a stream
The soft, green grass my pillow
Within, a warm daydream
The sound of water singing
As contentedly I lay
Great pleasure, to me bringing
Washing all my cares away
Bubbling round each mossy stone
Dancing with, each swaying reed
Then a subtle change of tone
Where, stream life, on algae feed
Splash, and whirl, come equally
In-between, each gentle sigh
Nature's soothing melody
A murmuring lullaby
An overture, feather-light
Carried on the summer air
A prelude to the river's might
As it gains momentum there
A preview quite hypnotic
In its sweet gentility
So pleasantly narcotic
A miniature symphony!

Patricia Whittle

THE PHONE STILL RINGS
(In loving remembrance of a dear brother and friend)

Sometimes, when I'm feeling blue,
The phone will ring - I'll think it's you.
I'll think of things I want to say,
Of things that make or mar my day.
Must tell you this - must tell you that,
The latest antics of my cat,
The little things, I've lately found
That help to make my world go round.
No more, your dear familiar voice
Will answer - help me make a choice.
We'll miss your smile, miss your dear face,
But know you're in a better place.
Go softly, Brother - warm and kind,
Remember those you've left behind.
For you'd not want to see us sad,
Please give my love to Mum and Dad.
God bless you - 'bye for now'.

Hilda Jones

IT'S FAIR TIME

Come to the thrill of the fair.
Puffs of candyfloss to share.
Stalls of silver and gold.
Sticky toffee apples to lick and hold.
Tents puffed up like mushroom tops.
Rides coloured like peppermint rocks
With red and white stripes.
Rows upon rows of glowing lights
Screams turn to laughter while we're flying high.
Faster and faster, faces whizzing by.
Some rides go up and then down
Or dizzy whirling round and round.
Dip and dive makes me feel woozy inside.
Don't forget to try a roller coaster ride.
So much fun without a doubt.
Even though it makes us scream and shout.
Legs feel funny like a jelly half-set
You bet.
Coo, what a sight!
Try not to look down, just hold on tight.
See jolly fairman with a toothy grin.
Roll up, roll up, three balls to win.
Don't like a camel, get the hump if you lose
There are plenty more stalls and prizes to choose
Even the moon seems to waltz with the stars
And join in the fun of the fair so delightful
As tasting candy in jars.

M A Hammer

DIVORCE

They say they love my brother and me,
Dad, Mum, her boyfriend, all three!
If they do, how could this be?
Friday, now is Dad's for tea,
Weekdays, with Mum we have to be,
They are getting divorced you see,
First we thought we were to blame,
Life will never be the same,
We'd be a family, surely we would,
If my brother and I had been good.

Mum's boyfriend, we like a lot,
We know a friend in him we've got,
And get on together very well,
But our Dad, we never tell!
He does not take it very well,
Both of us, we love our dad,
Divorce, has made him very sad,
We all liked it as we were,
Before divorce caused a stir.

Mum's boyfriend, was Dad's best mate,
Someone Dad will never hate!
For being together it's too late,
A time is set, so is the date,
Mum and Dad do not shout,
Together, they have worked it out
Divorce papers came through our door,
We are not a family anymore,
And our future is unsure.

Sheila Walters

STABLE STAR

Silver star, above the stable,
In sleepy Bethl'em town.
Showing humble shepherds, where the king without a crown,
Could be found so sweetly sleeping,
In a manger lined with hay.
Silver star above the stable
Please shine on us today.

As your light shone on that stable,
Those many years ago.
So let it gleam and twinkle, to let the whole world know
The King of Peace is with us,
At this joyous Christmastide.
His love will fill our hearts again,
And peace with us all abide.

Cynthia Byrnes

SQUIRRELS

Happy squirrels red and grey
Run and jump and climb all day
Should we get a climbing frame
And with practice do the same?

H Atkinson

THE FAIRY RING

Tiny fairy lanterns shine among the trees
Tinkling sounds of voices echo in the breeze
You think I must be dreaming, you smile and pinch yourself
And suddenly you see him, a tiny little elf.

He's dressed in yellow trousers, his jacket is bright red
He wears a silver waistcoat and a hat upon his head
If you are very careful and follow close behind
Along the path he's treading, a fairy ring you'll find.

You must be very quiet, do not make a sound
And you will find a magic place with fairies all around
Dressed in pink and lavender, yellow, blue and green
And seated on a toadstool the fairy king and queen.

Their wings are lightest gossamer, their clothes are silken lace
They smile and bless their fairy folk then slowly leave the place
Then tiny elves and fairies wait patiently in line
While fat and furry bumblebees serve honeysuckle wine.

You rub your eyes in disbelief, you can't believe it's true
When suddenly the fairies are looking straight at you
You whisper do not be afraid I come to do no harm
They do not seem to understand and flutter with alarm.

Sadly all at once they leave, you're standing all alone
In the golden fairy ring sad and so forlorn.
Each time you see a woodland this enchanted place you'll find
But only if you do not think, was it simply in my mind.

Diane L Brown

YOU ARE
(For Jane)

You're the words in all my songs
You're the right in all my wrongs
You're the joy in all my sadness
You're the good in all my badness.

You're the love in all this hate
You're the right time when all is late
You're the stars in life's dark skies
You're the beauty in my eyes.

You're the listening ear when all is loud
You're the silver lining in my cloud
You're the sweetest lily in any valley
You're the first with love when the rest tally.

You're the pick me up when I'm down
You're the one, the sad man's clown
You're the rock in times of strife . . .

So here's to the one I owe my life.

Lamb

CAT-ASTROPHE

Cats, cats, they drive you bats
They are in your hair and under your hats
And also on the rugs and chairs
And in the cupboards and on the stairs

When mealtimes come and they are fed
There's bound to be one in your bed
Who hasn't heard the call for tea
But turns up prompt at half-past three!

Ah puss, you are a pure delight
When stretched before the firelight
All peace and quiet in the hall
Until they hear the mating call
Then ears and whiskers all agog
Could it be the neighbour's dog?
With yowls and screams you cannot bear
You hide behind the kitchen chair
Only to find it's not your cats
Just some screeching owl or bats

Oh moggies, moggies everywhere
Curled on rugs or sat on chairs
What is it when I say, 'Oh drat'
Can't help but love those darned old cats.

Maureen Digges

A Reason To Believe

We all can live from day to day, each person bides time to achieve,
Within their own ability, a valued reason to believe.
All life must have some purpose, an inner need we all pursue
To gain our own perspective, fulfil your heart, compose a view.

Create an inner vision, a mirage you wish to obtain
For wasted time without a goal, another year you've lived in vain.
Nurture all that life can give, cherish all which you perceive
Trust your own ability, do not give blame and hence deceive.

There's truth within perspective, a pride in which we all can see
So strive to be the best you can, create your life with dignity.
Accept no one is perfect, keep in view an open mind
Give pain and grief through disrespect, then hence in turn that's all
you'll find.

Mistakes and heartaches come around without this turmoil you will
not see,
To cherish all the good you've found and face life with reality.
Reflect on which has passed with fate, redeem the dreams and wishes
too, life's too short to always hate
Hold on to all who stand by you.

Sometimes respect and showing love, may not denote to how you care,
Just remember those that gave you life, will not always in time be there.
With fate there is no justice when you live from day to day
Hold pride and hurt we all can miss expressing things we all should say.

Each sole is very special, one lifetime you have to achieve
You are given life endorsed by love,
You have a reason to believe.

Jane L Smith

THE TRAGEDY OF MONTECASSINO

Our visit to Montecassino left an impression so bold
As I sat quietly a story started to unfold
Two nations at war, each fighting to win
And what happened at that time was a terrible sin
The Abbey of Montecassino was held by one side
And was destroyed by the other, they had nowhere to hide
In just three hours it was reduced to rubble
Being a religious building they never expected trouble

The Abbey was rebuilt after the war
Back to its splendour, as it was before
Brick by brick, column by column
Bit by bit they covered the deed so solemn
It would be hard to describe the beauty and grace
Or the serenity you feel in this Holy place
They replaced the paths and gardens to all their glory
So it would seem a happy ending to such a sad story

Though buildings can be rebuilt, sadly lives can not
And at the bottom of this mountain we made another stop
This time to a cemetery full of monuments of stone
And to me this is where the real tragedy is shown
Young men in their prime fought hard and true
The British and their allies, the Polish and the Germans too
Soldiers and airmen but more important dads and sons
The victims of war, killed by bombs and guns.

Celia Law

A BALLAD OF LOVE

There once was a girl who harboured a dream
That fortune and fame would be hers one day
Her voice was renowned and held in esteem
She sang from the heart with words to convey.

Her dream reoccurred, the glory seemed real
The sound of applause remained in her head
How could she foresee, what fate would reveal
Love came along, soon ambition was dead.

They basked in their love, fulfilling each hour
Nothing else mattered, their joy was complete
The boy's love soon waned, and died like a flower
The girl grieved in vain, for what had been sweet.

Now older and wise, she recounts the cost
And sings a sad song, of love that was lost.

Margaret Wilson

FRUSTRATION

From the regions of my mind
Recollecting days gone by
Unravelling, the happenings,
Secrets, long lost, I will find
Times we had, when young and free,
Return, recalled, from memory.
Again, I see in my mind's eye
Things we did, time we spent.
Interesting places, we went.
Obstructions, frustrations still my pen,
Now writer's block is back again.

Marjorie Grant

HEARTFELT WISH

How I wish for peace in the world,
For some formula to be unfurled
To save us from war
And give hope from afar.

How can we stem our fears?
Or hold back our tears?
When aggression rules
It makes us all fools
With no will to say
'We need peace today'!

Why do we exist
Amid hate and raised fist?
Why rush into a fight
Fuelling temper and spite?
Has common sense flown
To a sphere unknown?

Who is brave enough to care,
To stand alone and dare
To nourish humanity
Within stark reality?

Bombs and guns are no answer,
Instead, create a limited spur
To suffering and destruction,
Horror, death and ruction.
Some way must be found
To create hope and peace all around,
For a change of heart now
To save mankind, *but how?*

S J Dodwell

PINING

I pine for you everyday
I pine for you in every way
I pine for you even when you are near
I pine for you when you're not here
I pine for you in the darkness of night
I pine for you in the bright sunlight
I pine for you when you're far away
I pine for you when you're here to stay
I pine for you as I walk alone
I pine for you when you don't phone
I pine for you when summer's here
I pine for you in winter drear
I pine for you in spring and autumn too
I wonder, will I always pine for you?

Ruth Howard

WHAT VALUE

What value a poem, in the world of today?
Or is this an answer, in truth we can't say!

Do we take enough time, to sit quiet and read,
To have a short break, surely something we need,
In our busy lives schedule, with cell phones or E-mail,
Do we aside all our problems, any meetings curtail?

I don't think we do, well, perhaps not enough,
We pretend we're resilient, alert and quite tough,
Nor do we give in, to ailments or aches,
For these in our timetable, inefficiency makes.

We 'commute' to work now, don't travel anymore,
Our days are more stressful than ever before,
Road traffic too, has increased many times,
Small wonder that 'road rage' features in crimes.

Remember when computers, were just distant dreams,
When we had chains of management, not efficiency teams.
We had time to read poetry, word pictures revealing,
We relaxed much more then, 'twas a time more appealing.

Yes, then we had time, for a life outside work,
Finding time to read poems, made us upwards to perk!
To become quite enraptured, with description or scene,
Be a hero or heroine, a king or a queen.

So . . . what value a poem? I'll ask once again,
Perhaps the answer's it eases our stresses and strain!

Jay Smith

AUTUMN LEAVES

In autumn, now the leaves are falling,
We surely hear our Saviour calling.
'Ye who are weary, follow me
For your salvation I will be'.
He alone can be our guide
Mocked, derided, crucified.
To save mankind, for us He died.
But was His sacrifice for nought?
He who Heaven and Earth has wrought
And with His blood mankind has bought?
In our sad world His word derided
By personal gain, man's strength decided
Was His sacrifice in vain
The Son of God, for sinners slain?
Holy Lord, come lead us on
To the place where thou hast gone -
Grant great compassion to the lowly
Our one Redeemer, Lord most holy.

Marcella Pellow

MY COOKER

My cooker is electric, it has always favoured me
It's been with us for many years we get on famously
I've never had a tearful day, I get such good results
Serving up exotic meals on time without fault

For most important menus it toils so happily
Unlike other implements it functions perfectly
When the family comes to dinner it has to be precise
For being quite efficient is very good advice

For parties and weddings she works like a slave
Never complaining, she does not sulk or rave
People sing her praises as they taste her pies
They love her roast and veggies and apple surprise

She has catered for many tastes from England and abroad
The compliments are many, it's what they can afford
But come the day of parting I know I'll shed a tear
For she has been my great companion year by year.

Barbara Tunstall

EASTER DAY

Now once more the glorious Easter tide
When we worship by each other's side.
And so we come with one intent
To share in the Easter Sacrament.
Christ is here, new risen to light,
To lift from woe to rapturous delight.
The bread and wine waiting to be blest.
Thick ardent lilies with high-holden crests
Upon the altar by the cross displayed
With resplendent silver all arrayed.

Around the church the ledges embrace
A fragile masterpiece, each flower in place,
A coloured weave never twice the same
To the risen Christ is laid again.
Offering in shape and colour for sight
To touch the mind with living light.
So with Alleluia voices raise
To the risen Christ a song of praise.
So that awe might properly overlay
The sights and sounds of this Easter Day.

Idris Woodfield

THE WHEEL OF LIFE

How can we justify our journey here,
Or is it part of a predestined plan
Decided for us in another sphere
Which also allocates our earthy span?

Once we are on life's ever-turning wheel
We quickly grow and learn to mix and play;
We do not stop to question or appeal
Against our fate or look beyond today.

When we are young there are so many things
To see and to absorb through dazzled eyes;
There are mistakes to make, and reckonings
Before we can be thought mature and wise.

The struggle to achieve exacts a price
With childhood innocence the sacrifice.

Rosina Winiarski

A VOLCANO

A twisted curl of greyish smoke does rise
From out the crater, wafted to the skies.
It looks so innocent, slight and serene
That some forget what that pale smoke does mean.
That mountain vast with rocky, bouldered sides
Deep in some nether cavern evil hides,
And in those darkest depths and murky pits
A drowsy spirit at this moment sits.
How long will he remain in this calm mood?
And sullenly o'er all his kingdom brood?
Soon will his anger rise against the world
And he'll leap up, his fiery banners furled.
Out from the yawning chasm belching forth
Will come his servants in their power and wrath.
Boiling lava, steaming sulphur, all
Mixed with rocks, that leaping up do fall
And down the steep sides rush at headlong rate
In jumbled mass and terrifying state.
Then slowly does the rumbling roaring din
Get quieter, and settling down within
The spirit once more drowses there in peace
And calls upon his servants now to cease.
The sky appears to be of molten hue,
And down below the mountains changed, a view
Of naught save ashy lava, cracked and bare
Is seen, and ruin spreads round everywhere.
Just this is left, for as the evening dies
A twist of greyish smoke curls to the skies.

Hilary Large

AUTUMN

The mists of autumn steal silently through dew-kissed grass.
The sun rises slowly, a huge red mass.
Cartwheeled spiders' webs hang pearl-dropped in the hedgerows.
Purple heather turns to gold on the distant moors.
Leaves of russet and brown drift gently down the windless air
Leaving the trees stark and bare.
The overblown rose heads hang wearily down,
Long-legged gadflies dance around.
Birds gather noisily on telephone lines,
Preparing for long journeys to sunnier climes.
Bumblebees drone lazily round the last flowers,
A small red robin chirrups cheekily in the bower.
Farmers have long since gathered in the hay,
Church harvest festivals are well underway
Soon the north winds will blow
Heralding hoar frosts and drifting snow.

Dorothy Schofield

THIS IS MY JOB

I work with patients every day,
They come and go, come what may
To listen and care is their first need,
I love my job, yes, indeed

As time goes by and patients go,
To build a friendship from the first *'Hello'*
I'm no angel, I'm just me
I'm a caring person, of which you see

So as these friendships build each day
I come to work, come what may,
In rain or shine I have a smile
To see their face is so worthwhile

Illness does not discriminate between colour and creed,
For this I must fulfil my need
To care and listen that is my job,
From ward to ward I give a nod

A smile, a nod, is all it takes,
Some loving care, until day breaks
Until the darkness does disappear,
You'll be in hospital and I'll be near.

Sharon Christian

WAITING

When the earth is white and the sky is grey
It's hard to recall a summer's day
When the swallows dart, and the humming bee
Adds her dizzy song to life's melody.

(And a distant hum in a sapphire sky
As a lazy plane watched the world go by).

Yet it helps to know as grey days drag by
That it won't be long till we see a sky
Picture-framed by blooms on a cherry tree;
We'll hear once more Miss Busy Bee –
Smell fresh-mown grass and scented flowers
Have time to while away the hours
And bless each precious hour that we
Can tuck inside our memory.

Hannah Yates

ANIMAL – TAME AND FERAL

Animals, big or small, insects or reptiles, birds or fish.
I think that they are amazing things,
To own lots of animals is my one true wish,
The most amazing animals are the ones with wings.

My two favourite animals are cats and dogs,
They are both extremely good fun,
I even like little toads and frogs,
My two dogs are father and son.

Many animals can be seen at the zoo,
A greater collection cannot be found,
There are tigers, giraffes, and elephants too
Monkeys make a terrible sound.

The panda, cute and cuddly, they may seem
But no other animal will dare take them on
They eat bamboo and drink from the stream
What a pity they're nearly all gone.

Cats, they are wonderful little pets,
They rub round you lovingly and sleep in your lap,
They don't like going to the vet's
My cat even likes to drink out of the tap.

Sarah Lemin (14)

IN OCTOBER THE CLOCKS GO BACK ONE HOUR

An extra hour, what could we do?
Well, maybe write a line or two
Stay in bed for an earned lie-in
Or empty the overflowing bin

We could clean the windows or dust the hall
Collect the fallen leaves on the soggy lawn
Curl up cosy with a real good book
Or stay in the kitchen and learn to really cook

Be a lounge lizard in front of the old TV
Visit a friend we've meant to see
Have a soak in the bath, what a pleasure
We should all find more time for leisure

We could phone a mate or write that letter
Ask that sick pal if she's feeling better
Take a long walk in the local woods
Watch the wildlife, if only we could

Listen to music, whatever the taste
Life is full of so much haste
I've a whole hour extra today
But it seems to have just flitted away.

Christina B Cox

TATTOOED EYES

Did you find it yet?
Did you find what you've been looking for?
I only ask 'cos I'm not sure
You never seem to smile no more
And you wear your hat so low
How am I to know?
Did you find it yet?
Did you find what you've been looking for?
Did you find the face behind the door?
The perfect face you had before
And was it worth the price you paid
For that stupid hit parade?
Did you find it yet?
Did you find what you've been looking for?
You gotta broken heart, a broken jaw
And the smallest nose I ever saw
They really cut you down to size
With all their pretty lies
Did you find it yet?
Did you find what you've been looking for?
I only ask 'cos I'm not sure
You never seem to smile no more
All alone in your disguise
God help you
And God bless your tattooed eyes!
God help you
And God bless your tattooed eyes!

Rod Trott

ENGLISH ROSE

Oh English Rose with petals so red
like all the soldiers whose blood was shed
they fought to keep our country free
their blood was given for you and me

Old English Rose you smell divine
held in my hand this giving time
I think of all those who have perished
Oh English Rose you are so cherished

Oh English Rose with buds so tight
whose fragrant flower is in sight
help me keep grateful for their blood shed
with open petals of blood-red

Oh English Rose don't wilt and die
in case we ask the reason why
so many people died to keep us free
with your red petals looking up at me

M Dodd

SANTA'S BIG TASK

Santa wears a red coat,
So just write him a note,
And maybe he'll bring what you ask.
Then just close your eyes,
And you'll get a surprise,
Though Santa has got a *'big'* task.

He lives in a cave,
And he'll give you a wave,
And laugh *'Ho-ho'* when he's jolly.
But watch as you go,
If you're naughty, he'll know,
He'll be angry, if he sees, silly folly.

He'll ride on his sleigh,
Early on Christmas Day,
And may bring you lovely presents.
So be very good,
As you know you should,
And don't annoy your parents.

Martin Snowdon

MATERNITY

As you go on maternity leave
With a belly so big you can hardly breathe
With an aching back and swollen feet
Struggling to cope in the summer heat
To endure the offerings of daytime TV
Sample the delights of Richard and Judy
Antenatal scans and bloods, oh, what fun
Waiting for the big day to come
And when you hold baby in your arms
Succumb to their baby charms
Their tiny face with eyes so bright
You won't mind the endless, sleepless nights.

Jackie Manning

Rhodes

Where blue is blue and green is green
The jealousy of man is rarely seen
His hand outstretched across the land
To reach her body in the golden sand.

Tracey Callison

SKIN-DEEP!

Orchids, roses – and hollyhocks
Stately homes – and girls in frocks
All these things – hold beauty deep
Some go to extremes – their attraction to keep
With knives, lasers – or plastered with paint
They suffer alteration – to make onlookers faint
Exuding their toys – to tempt the boys
Lifting and changing – all effort employs
They grow, they know – there seems little doubt
That looks on the surface – out loud will shout
'I *am* I *will* – God will above'
Spread my wings to bring to me some love
To fly on high – to maybe catch the eye
I am meant to tempt – to make the boys sigh
But when age meets sage – it is a fact
That good *cooks* not *looks* – do most attract
Though the bloom may fade – a good meal made
Is far more attractive – than diamond, ruby or jade
No need for the knife – ask any wise wife
A satisfied stomach – holds attention for life
With love, some shove – and expertise
One can bring anything like a husband – to his knees
Good wife, no strife – no beauty deep
Don't be a dope – with hope – a good man you can keep.

John L Wright

SCOTLAND

Dazzling droplets sparkling gems
Over the moors down to the glens
Still is the mist waiting winds call
Serenely vast heathers to curtsy and fall
Quietly springs escape from the earth
Reaching a point with ferocity and mirth

Lost are the memories beneath virgin snow
For nature reclaims which was once long ago
Where rowan and fungi are as red as the fire
Colours of each clan's spectacular attire
Eerie sounds of pipes mingle with the breeze

As chieftains and men camped beneath trees
History and blood buried in this land
Blue lochs hide their secrets as in a fisted hand
Wander with passion and lust of free men
Feel in your heart the songs of the glens.

Susan E Roffey

MANY BROKEN MINDS

Along the rail before the crowd
Stood men in khaki tall and proud
Across the oceans they must sail
Where enemy fire falls like hail
On foreign shore they made their stance
To be cut down with little chance
Now England needs to save a friend
Each little boat she'll call and send
Across the oceans cold and wide
Flotilla rode on every tide
'Bring them home' was England's cry.
'Twas our mistake, don't let them die
They struggled on to those in reach
To set them down on English beach
Many watched a comrade fall and die
Then stood alone to reason why
Yet struggled on with weary back
Loyal to King and Union Jack
In their pain and tormented sorrow
Lay the path to freedom
We may have tomorrow
Many broken minds still pain today
God bless them all
For what they had to pay.

Brian Wardle

TRAINS OF THOUGHT

Travelling cramped
Spirit is damped
Don't meet their eyes
Too much surprise
Radio ears
Lips on their beers
Feeling like sleep
Just take a peep
See dirty look
Hide in my book
Four hours have passed
We're here at last!
Just want to shout
Please let me out!
Oooh . . . Oooh . . .

Anita Layland

THE WATCHER

From dark shadows you called out to the world,
Creeping within the tangled paths of its mind,
Lingering; to see if it heard your cry.
A cry made only by your gentle kind.

Lonely, you were the only soul to breathe
The wondrous air of freedom, love and peace
As you pranced on crisp autumnal leaves.
But still your desperate pleading never ceased.

The world was deafened by greed and pain,
Blinded by hate, deceit and when it stopped
To take account of what was lost, then –
And only then – did it know you had watched,

For someone said they'd heard your call
But no one will find you now – sweet Unicorn.

Margaret Newbold

GOODNIGHT MY DARLING

Goodnight my darling, it is time for us to part,
And we will see each other tomorrow,
Never to leave each other with a broken heart.
Parting is such sorrow.
As a tear comes to my eye,
I don't want to leave you on your own,
Tears running down my cheeks as I cry.
And leave you all alone.
We shall wait until tomorrow,
Till we see each other again,
And there will be no more sorrow.
When I am with you, you drive me insane.
One day my darling, we will be married,
Over the threshold, you will be carried.

Tina Rooney

BLUE SUEDE SHOES

In innocent serenities of blue
peacocks shirr their psychedelic tails,
as you, the virile Elvis we once knew
shirred out the notes of diatonic scales.

So many eyes on you, in the spotlights' glare,
where young girls screamed before you played one chord
you came, you conquered: yes, we do still care
although your life became so deeply flawed.

For sadly, innocence destroyed by fame
left you less a peacock, more a jay.
Yet some still hold your burnt-out flaring flame
re-lit, now sees the kindling light of day,

Shines on your blue suede shoes hung out to dry
beneath the spotlights of some other sky.

Norman Meadows

THE BIOLOGIST

I puzzle out your letters – try to weave
Your life from them, your science and your art;
Discoveries, contentions interleave
Combine to form the story I impart.

I reach to you across 100 years
And strain to grasp your essence, how you were
Your feelings, your successes and your fears
Some half-discovered, others I infer.

The first draft's done, five volumes on the shelf
Bound in maroon, their silken bookmarks hang
And now the second draft I set myself
Improve the song that I already sang,

Breathe life into the thinker and his thought
The battles won and lost, so bravely fought.

Rosemary D Harvey

GENIUS

It is a genius of a day, with hands held firm
on helms. The race gun booms across the bay.
In sympathy with the flowing sea, the stern
wakes of altered courses trace the race away.

The sails billow and fill. Contenders sight the sea
reaching for the sky above, as the winds prevail
upon the sails to hold their breath on the lee;
as the boards tremor in expectation of the trail.

Keels part their depths. Waves slice their bows.
The buoys go about the hazards of the helm.
The crossing line measured by the ambition of vows
crowned by the bonding in the matrix of their realm.

Wherever there may be endeavour, in work or play,
the Genius of the Universe transcends the day.

Michael Alan Fenton

SONNET TO AN ENGLISH LAKE

The summer breeze had wafted round the green,
the lake shone smooth just like an antique board
that had been polished to a deep, deep sheen
and gleams, as coins in a golden hoard.
No ripple mars the surface, even fish
are deep below and somnolent with heat.
A single dragonfly on wings a'swish
now flits from reed to reed, with movements neat,
to find that special one down which to creep
and lay her precious eggs upon its stem.
Although there seems no wind up which to keep
a thistledown seed, floating like a gem,
rising on high, caught by the setting sun.
A Nightjar tells the world that day is done.

D G W Garde

LIFE'S DILEMMA

There is in life dilemma
Twists and turns and holes
And I ask myself will I ever
Get peace of mind, body and soul?

It is such a lot to ask
Maybe it will never be
But the one to perform the task
Yes, my dear friend, is me

Err on the side of caution
Relax, take time and space
There surely is a portion
Of happiness in this place

And if my choice is a mistake
Then I shall just accept my fate!

Tricia Layton

WEATHERING THE STORM

The roar of the waves upon the shore,
Rang within my shell-like ears,
Moaning, moaning, until I could take no more,
And so I fled, tasting the salty tears.

Now from afar I looked again,
Saw grey clouds lash the sky,
Saw forked light, cause her pain,
Heard her constant, rumbling, woeful cry,

I felt her sorrow, I too cried,
Our tears mingled, upon the sand,
As we waited for the storm to subside,
Hearts and souls united, woman and land,

We found strength, from devastation,
Knowing soon, we would find elation.

Clare Allen

LET ME SPEAK OF MY LOVE

I know you do not love me and I blame you not for this:
But your love is no less sought, nor my heart less true
Because my hair is dullish brown, my eyes a weakish blue;
My nose is not so dainty - my mouth no thing to kiss.
How cruel of Mother Nature to deny me beauty's bliss!
She's blessed the clueless bud and the pointless morning dew,
The hidden fish's fin and the unseen mountain view.
Yes! Heartless Mother Nature and heartless you for this.

Now let me speak of *my* love - as wide as this Earth
With seven seas to bathe your tears, five lands to offer rest;
But what need hath *you* for gentle shores and easy, dulling surf
When starry maids in passion's brightest colours dressed
Do twirl and tempt with endless beauty, charm and mirth -
To offer the treasure you covet when my true heart is best.

Julia M Glenn

THE SWANS

I eye your eye, primeval, I hiss with hate,
You sigh, with my beauty, with elation,
I move your very soul, to there create,
A moving ancient prayer of rare creation.

I glide through river's tidal streams of light,
I, silhouetted, in leadership of love,
Symmetry, nature's elemental fight.
When I snake my neck, you're detrimental.

With love I bring my cygnets close to you,
Showing my newborn friends with such delight,
Eating your crust and drinking river's dew,
To teach and bear my young in newborn sight.

Listen, when I descend from the stars above,
Know, I the swan die with my mate, of love.

Elizabeth Rose French

MANNEQUIN

Your loveliness is beyond compare
Such is the credit to your sex
I would not touch or even dare
Your beauty being so exquisite
You were designed so wondrously
Then to this earth you were bestowed
A goddess of gentility it radiates and shows
In a department store window draped you glow
So many notice this grand illusion
As they clamour to the windowpane
Causing such chaos and utter confusion
As the law books so many names

Alas you are removed and taken far away
Finding you on a scrap heap to my home you will stay.

R D Hiscoke

FOOD FOR THOUGHT

Feasting on pheasant (bleak mid-winter's treat),
an old tooth shatters on concealed lead shot.
Cross at the loss (and dental cost!) I eat -
ruminating upon the poor bird's lot -

and, as my fork picks bare his fragile bones,
imagine him again in wondrous flight,
and know that I (for whom God's Lamb atones)
am one with him who shares a mortal plight:

he from his covert soars towards the sun,
I sanguinely from savage schooldays climb;
he brightly in his pride is felled by gun,
I by some dread disease am downed in time.

The Lord of Life once gave us for our need
His Son. Some killed Him; others on Him feed.

Bernard Brown

LOVE
(The Italian sonnet)

Is the heart of our emotion?
Reality to unravel the hypnotic
Social accepted flirt is erotic
Exerts the cause for commotion
Bewitched the spell of potion
Cruel deception bordering the psychotic
True life measures the exotic
Adored forever in lotion

Endless caress in blissful passion
So simple so pure and true
Cloaked in a world of fashion
Eyes of burning ashes turn blue
Instant elusion for attraction
Love my sole renew

Joyce

I WISH

I wish the world could live in peace today
Without the doubts and hate within our heart
To try to talk and meet each one half-way
And not to fight and tear our lives apart.

Within your heart you plant a seed of love
And then you watch it grow and so, to bloom
If you can heed the words of God above
And help to chase away these clouds of gloom.

Each night I sit upon my bed and pray
Dear Lord just speak to those who start a war
Give them a sign to stop without delay
To bring us peace on earth I do implore.

You have the strength to pass it on down here
That we may live our life without this fear.

Gladys Baillie

MY FIGHT FOR FREEDOM

When the war broke out I was just thirteen,
The word 'teenager' not yet invented,
In those days regarded as an 'in-between',
Acting grown-up, I really resented!

The restricting underclothes women wore -
Tight suspender belt and thick, lisle stockings,
To my tomboyish ways, a complete bore,
Appalled me with a threat all too shocking!

Thank goodness for a silk stocking shortage,
Even though my seams will never be straight,
I'll resort to wear them in my dotage,
I hope, by then, my legs have lost some weight.

After the war ended, I was twenty
And wearing precious nylons a-plenty!

Olive Miller

WATERMILL

Watermill by the flowing stream,
Rushes growing, yellow water lilies flowering,
Ponies in paddocks grazing, grey heron fishing,
Ducks paddling, shoals of morning bream;
Dragonfly exploring the flowing water,
Blackberries ripening in hedgerows,
Like arrows loosened from longbows,
Swallows circle above the willow river;
Stile onto the meadow path, meadow flowers,
Roost of nocturnal bats spinning,
An old, hollow oak tree towers,
Cattle to milking, maid singing;
Mill upon the River Stour,
Carter arrives to collect the flour.

Janet Eirwen Smith

LOVE'S ENDING

There is a thing I've learnt at cost
That magic moments have disappeared
The dreams we dreamed are lost
Maybe they were not as they appeared

Awakening the heart to love
Is a very precious thing
All feelings are soft as a dove
My sadness is all in remembering

Often I sense our first kiss
As an autumn leaf fell
To float upon the river, my wish
This now is our autumn of life, farewell

How fast a flow becomes a stream
Then on love goes as if it's never been

Elizabeth Cowley-Guscott

RIVERS FLOW

Rivers flow all through the night
Never weary or tired they be
Curling, twisting from morn till night
On a journey to meet the sea.

Seems to me a miracle
Rivers never lose their way
Curling, twisting o'er same stony track
Flowing on night and day.

How nice to follow a river
Through valleys, glens and braes
To walk along the riverbank see the ripples glitter
Where wild ducks nest among stately reeds that sway.

Follow a river along the way on its journey to the sea
Serene inspiring journey, a rugged journey maybe.

Frances Gibson

SONNET ONE

I think of nothing else but your sweet lips,
Yet you know nought of my true love for thee,
My broken heart is torn from tip to tip,
Although I know that love can never be.

To me you are an angel from above,
Yet silent will I always now remain,
I think of you as my soft feather'd dove,
Now that I know I ne'er shall be thy swain,

The love I feel is penance I shall bear,
To gaze on you is all that I can ask,
If you will deign on me a smile to cast,
To lighten every day my daily task.

My life is bound to yours, yet you know not,
And I can find strange joy in all my lot.

John Whittock

IRISH ISLE BALLAD

'O' Irish isle' the seagulls cry
Your people have gone astray.
The hatred between religions festers every day
Behind closed doors the families sit at night,
No family fun, only talk of 'Strife, strife, strife!'
The hatred boils in everyone,
It's carried down the line.
It really amazes me where you get the time,
To throw those bombs, to fight those fights.
How can you even sleep at night?
All you do is make your children 'Weep, weep, weep'
O' Ireland, land of fairs, song and dance,
Join your hands together and give your children a chance.
You're in your grave a long, long time. You're dead for evermore.
Your children will weep when you are gone.
The hatred will live forever more.
Will it keep going down the line?
'O' Ireland,' the seagulls cry.

Ellen Pauler Ewart

FINDING SPACE FOR LOVE

The first time I encountered love there was
A narrow single bed for us to share
And it was something beautiful because
I held her in my arms with room to spare

Now often since it's never quite matched up
Or offered that same open-handed space
At best, the bounty of a half-filled cup
At worst, a night beside a scornful face

So precious then the one who smiles and winks
More valuable than gold to fill my hands
That friend who never counts the cost, or thinks
Of pacing out dimensions in the sands

When all is told, there is no greater prize
Than coming home to warm and loving eyes

David Gasking

RESOLUTION

I'm ever staring at myself, with gaze,
It is the hand of fate I, to me, cast,
It seems I cannot reach those happy days,
Nor can I touch the joy, is in the past.
I am a silhouette under the light,
Time's passing and I have nothing to give,
The blackness is awash, removes my sight,
I am an empty shell, no will to live.

A spark of hope remains inside me still,
Within the sacred jar, it did not die,
I must remove the lid, let fire fill,
Ignite and end each weary, soulful sigh.
Will do away with all the pain and strife,
So I can once again enjoy my life.

Jillian Shields

PHOENIX IN ENGLISH MODE

In times like this it's hard to see the light,
To think our world will ever be the same,
When fears and thoughts haunt the mind at night.
As those tall towers fell to enemy flame.
Those pictures play on every TV screen,
The news is recycled and repeated,
We cannot escape the disaster scene
Or avoid the many words to be read.

Thoughts move to less distressing domains,
A phoenix, the city returns to life.
We shuffle on, take up forgotten reins,
Move on despite our lingering inner strife.

From now on, good not evil rules the skies,
From those ashes, a new courage did arise.

Janet M Baird

IN A BOOK SENT TO HIS BELOVED

The book I send you, think it is my friend
    Who comes to speak for me with one so fair
And will my lack of qualities amend
    By his own worth, which he would gladly share.
Who would be other than a friend to me
    Who shared with me so many hours of joy,
Who so delighted with his company
    And did for pastime his choice gifts employ?
Fear not to take him - there was never friend
    Who could betray me less, or serve me more;
No king did ever such a legate send
    Who better did his secret counsel store.
No friend have I more trusted than this book:
    Read and find pleasure whensoe'er you look.

Barrie Williams

PRECIOUS HOURS

Gather your thoughts for we know
They will disappear into the night
Take in each moment as they ebb and flow
Precious hours too soon taking flight

Gather your thoughts before they are gone
Make memories of all your days
Share each from now on
The hours to years fly in a haze

Gather your thoughts too soon we forget
Of all the things that are past
There is time for regret
Live for today and make everything last

Life's precious hours
We gather as flowers

Jeanette Gaffney

AWESOME

Deepest oceans dark, hidden, illusive mystery
Surfs, crazed breakers, wild demons ever rolling
Lashing torrents, surge, mighty, mighty sea
Witchcraft stirs, savage spells cajoling
Violence, turning, ebbing, waning, wanton dashing
Icy cold waves, caress, ghoulish secrets deep
Roaring, screaming, sea world, blindly crashing
Satan's arms, embrace, salty, deathly sleep
Fraying phantoms drink pungent tasting rain
Tormented ghosts cascade great vapoured bladder
Natives' wildest deluge, a heaving, monstrous strain
Seafaring angels climb waterfall's mighty ladder
Masterful temptress, disturbing, beauty embracing
Wondrous creation, Mother Nature onward racing

Ann Hathaway

TRUE LOVE

In our modern world love is too absent,
Strong men control, dictate, consume and hate.
Somehow, true love has to grace the present,
Even if to most, it appears too late.
Women possess, at heart, a love so fierce
And such true love should not be kept hidden.
Its strong power mighty armour can pierce
To make the strongest man do as bidden.
This strength of love we are giving no chance;
Such a female love needs to be set free,
That we may all perceive true love advance.
Hand in hand, then, with God's love shall we see
A true love, not so weak, thus make progress
To a new world of peace and success.

Susan Audrey

LOVE IS -

Some would say that love is dead
the purpose has gone, there's only despair,
when resentment and bitterness fill the head
and the world's to blame - it's so unfair!

Some would say that love is 'one way'
and material things take the place,
true feelings are destroyed each day,
then reality and greed show their face.

Some would say that love is all
when we share both tears and joy,
sometimes beaten, you can still walk tall
when the love in your heart you employ.

So said - my friends, it's no surprise,
that true love never, ever dies.

Alex Dickie

PEAKS OF FASHION

On bikes, large and small, they teem all about,
Phenomenal, the fashion, never doubt:
Certainly though, they can rarely have seen,
Far less to, a baseball match have they been,
Yet everyone's out in his funnelled peak!
Schooldays, holidays throughout ev'ry week,
Particularly so, those little chaps
Are ev'rywhere seen in those baseball caps,
But instantly barred from the social run
If buzzing around you're not sporting one!
Is it true they wear them in their beds
Mysteriously clinging to their heads?

On reaching their manhood, little surprise:
Simply a change to a different size!

Ron Hails

ANGELIAR

Tell me I'm an angel, higher,
Higher than a fallen mind.
Tell me that you are a liar.

Tell me there's no more to find,
Nothing exists beyond this life.
Tell me I'm an angel, higher.

Tell me this love is the lasting kind,
There is no truth in what can never die,
Tell me that you are a liar.

Tell me sanctity is still alive,
Until I believe beyond reprise,
Tell me I'm an angel, higher.

Tell me there are no more tears to cry
From eyes in purity wrung ever dry,
Tell me that you are a liar.

Tell me this will not pass me by,
That this motion carries on endless tide.
Tell me I'm an angel, higher,
Tell me that you are a liar.

Helen Marshall

SINGLE COMPLICATIONS

Now single creatures you and I
No shared bed, twinned thought hard to find
To separate ways our hopes now sadly fly

Our sharing now a long and distant sigh
Now, love's easy faith lingers far behind
Now single creatures you and I

For though a thought still stirs the eye
And though old ways invade the mind
To separate ways our hopes now sadly fly

Now what once was true is found a lie
And what once entwined has undermined
Now single creatures you and I

Days come now and too slowly die
As painful caution breeds ways now redefined
To separate ways our hopes now sadly fly

What once was we, we ask now why
That unleashed love, alas, is far behind
Now single creatures you and I
To separate ways our hopes now sadly fly.

Geoff Simpson

NE'ER A THOUGHT

You knocked me down and stood upon my dignity
I crouched in pain upon a bloodied floor
And then you strolled away with ne'er a thought of me

Your vitriolic footsteps tortured gleefully
They'll echo in my ears for evermore
You knocked me down and stood upon my dignity

Battered me with cruel insensitivity
You slowly turned and smiling, slammed the door
And then you strolled away with ne'er a thought of me

My heart was ripped apart by your duplicity
Believing in the love that you once swore
You knocked me down and stood upon my dignity

Surveyed my plight with ill-concealed perversity
My each and every plea, chose to ignore
And then you strolled away with ne'er a thought of me

Sitting here with nothing but the memory
My wounds, though hidden, still are raging sore
You knocked me down and stood upon my dignity
And then you strolled away with ne'er a thought of me.

Kim Montia

EARTH'S FIRST SPRING

What wonder was in the first spring;
When hills and valleys silent lay
Before the birds began to sing.

Earth waiting for the sun to fling
Gold through the misty silver-grey;
What wonder was in the first spring;

For little winds to rise and swing
The green arched branches starred with may
Before the birds began to sing.

For dew to dry and warmth to bring
Flowers' fragrance to the fields of day;
What wonder was in the first spring;

For clouds that to wild mountains cling,
Unveiling heights to drift away,
Before the birds began to sing.

For sweetest sounds through Earth to ring,
New music of a timeless lay;
Such wonder was in the first spring
As all the birds began to sing.

Diana Momber

GENTLE SILENCE

As night-time silence gently falls,
Dark shadows roam the slumbering land,
Into my dreams she softly calls.

Inside my room, midst sheltering walls,
Held safe in her protecting hands,
As night-time silence gently falls.

In darkness, demons, dragons crawl,
Try to invade but she has planned,
Into my dreams she softly calls.

Beside her beauty they are small,
Dwarfed by her shadow where she stands,
As night-time silence gently falls.

Such love as hers, how it enthrals,
So burns the flame of passion fanned,
Into my dreams she softly calls.

She whispers words, I hear them all,
In life we were as woven strands,
As night-time silence gently falls,
Into my dreams she softly calls.

Jim Sargant

PERFECT MATE

Maybe soon I'll find perfect mate,
Perhaps true love will pass me by,
Single life's sad to contemplate.

But I'm prepared to sit and wait,
Cannot attract men, though I try,
Maybe soon I'll find perfect mate.

Who'll turn up on time, not be late,
It's not fair, I hear myself cry,
Single life's sad to contemplate.

I'm fair of face, with shapely thigh,
But sob aloud, give a long sigh,
Maybe soon I'll find perfect mate.

With wavy hair or even straight,
Need someone to love or I'll die,
Single life's sad to contemplate.

Somewhere must be my ideal date,
Always expectation's been high,
Maybe soon I'll find perfect mate,
Single life's sad to contemplate.

S A Mullinger

VILLANELLE -
(Tears falling from a blood-red rose)

Tears falling from a blood-red rose
I look afar and sense the view
The blood is mine I must suppose

I clutch the flower, then I doze
Is it my fault or was it you?
Tears falling from a blood-red rose

How was it this disgust arose
I am betrayed, what will ensue?
The blood is mine I must suppose

I struggled, yet when heartache goes
Desire to harm can come to you
Tears falling from a blood-red rose

That rose, now white, in my heart froze
I'm sorry, for I did love you
The blood is mine I must suppose

Take comfort in your last repose
The rose has only drops of dew
Tears falling from a blood-red rose
The blood is mine I must suppose.

Ann Marriott

AS I SHALL ALWAYS LOVE YOU

As I shall always love you.
From that day when we first met -
And I thought you loved me, too!

My desire for you I guess you knew
And that my heart on you was set,
As I shall always love you.

I've kept wondering what I could do
And was this too good to be true?
And I thought you loved me, too!

Often at times I did this rue,
My constancy I did regret,
As I shall always love you.

Why was it that I you always drew,
But never, never I could get?
And I thought you loved me, too!

What has been keeping us apart - tell me who;
For you must know I do but fret,
As I shall always love you
And I thought you loved me, too!

Beatrice Wilson

THE ROYAL WAY

May wisdom bless enquiring minds
And touch the sage's heart
For he who seeks is he who finds

And as the spirit daily grinds
Found rutting as the noble hart
May wisdom seek enquiring minds

Then mating with the comely hinds
Eternal bonds of truth impart
For he who seeks is he who finds

Yet even on the road that winds
Where troubles pierce like a dart
May wisdom seek enquiring minds

Of all the secrets faith designs
The wise man plays his part
For he who seeks is he who finds

And not an oath more solemn binds
Than those of heaven's chart
May wisdom seek enquiring minds
For he who seeks is he who finds

Cherry

BEST KEPT IN A DRAWER

Ripped the paper heart today:
Crumpled spirit a single tear,
Fold it neat to put away

Love you, sad you love to play;
I long for you to miss me dear
Ripped the paper heart today

Fading warmth has slipped away,
Once constant now a stinging jeer,
Fold it neat to put away.

Your voice the music, I would sway;
A memory my heart adhere:
Ripped the paper heart today.

No longer with you I can lay,
Never again hold your hand I fear
Fold it neat to put away.

In my heart your face shall stay,
Your deep blue eyes in darkness clear:
Ripped the paper heart today,
Fold it neat to put away.

Lauren Elizabeth Wood

OH HEART OF MINE

Oh! Heart of mine, your love has pined,
I want to be with you,
But here I am and left behind.

We laughed, we joked, we wined and dined.
Have you thought this through?
Oh! Heart of mine, your love has pined!

Your heart to mine, I'll ever bind,
As I my heart to you.
But I am here and left behind!

I'll soldier on until I find
Someone to answer true.
Oh! Heart of mine, your love has pined.

I thought you to be true and kind,
As other lovers do.
But I am here and left behind.

As through life's journey I do wind,
And you will travel too,
Oh! Heart of mine, your love has pined,
But I am here and left behind!

Christine Nuttall

BROKEN WINGS

A bird of freedom once you flew
Over green meadows and treetops high
Ring-necked dove, so sad are you

Broken wings, tinged greyish blue
Feathered plumage, there you lie
A bird of freedom, once you flew

Safe sanctuary in garden's greenest view
From whence you came from sunnier skies
Ring-necked dove, so sad are you

Painful cry in silence coo
Suffering until the twilight's nigh
A bird of freedom, once you flew

In hour of need, beside you through
Gentle and soft, your looks belie
Ring-necked dove, so sad are you

When heaven calls, your time is due
Final exit, your demise and die
A bird of freedom, once you flew
Ring-necked dove, so sad are you

Rebecca Hart

THE TRAVELLER

Make fast the doors and shutters tonight!
The wind without howls cold and chill.
May God defend us 'til morning light.

The frost is keen; the stars are bright
Snow clouds are gathering o'er the hill.
Make fast the doors and shutters tonight!

There's a traveller nearing; the storm's at its height,
Welcome him in for board and bill,
May God defend us 'til morning light.

He is weary and weak, without guide or sight,
Having travelled far over field and rill.
Make fast the doors and shutters tonight!

He has spoken long of the need to live right
For the Lord, with His spirit afresh to fill,
May God defend us 'til morning light.

We know not his name, but by God's might
He has left with a blessing; may the storm be still.
Make fast the doors and shutters tonight!
May God defend us 'til morning light.

Joan Thompson

RECOFLECTION

Swifter than the clock's hands sweep
Around the span of all our days,
Time makes haste to bring us sleep.
More than all the thoughts we keep
On which our memories turn to graze,
Swifter than the clock's hands sweep
Through our fingers moments seep
As lifetimes go their separate ways.
Time makes haste to bring us sleep;
Though hours can drag, the years still leap
To disappear in memory's haze
Swifter than the clock's hands sweep.
Eventually we all must reap
The fruits, our routes through life shall raise.
Time makes haste to bring us sleep
In which we see 'neath waters deep
The sum of all our yesterdays.
Swifter than the clock's hands sweep
Time makes haste to bring us sleep.

Jonathan Goodwin

RIVER OF FORGETFULNESS

Is there a river of forgetfulness
A place to drink foreverness
A place to wash your life away
A place where there is no yesterday?

I wonder

Is there a life when life has gone?
Is there more? Do we carry on?
Where on Earth do we come from?

I wonder

In this river so clean and pure
Where a new life can mature
Is there really another door?

I wonder

A river of forgetfulness
It's a very nice idea
A river to wash away
All of the fear
A river where death
Is just a tear.

I wonder.

Deana Freeman

BLACKBIRD'S SONG

My heart lifts at your joyous trill
Heralding the dawn with ecstasy,
A magic song from golden bill.

Gradually the darkness fades until
I see my songster flying free,
My heart lifts at your joyous trill.

Your throat throbs as the notes distil,
Weaving a wondrous fantasy,
A magic song from golden bill.

You take my offerings, spurning nil,
You preen and bathe, then perch in tree,
My heart lifts at your joyous trill.

Just for a while you vanish till
As dusk creeps in so stealthily,
A magic song from golden bill.

Then once again your notes fulfil
My longing for your melody.
My heart lifts at your joyous trill,
A magic song from golden bill.

Roma Davies

A LITTLE BIT MORE

(Dedicated to Marian Mawson, died 1st November 2001 -
a little bit more than a friend)

A little bit more than a friend
A little bit more than a mother
You were always there to the end

How can this be the last letter penned
Please reconsider, recover
A little bit more than a friend

I want to believe that you're on the mend
I'll not overwhelm you nor smother
You were always there to the end

If I could give you my strength, I'd not lend
Don't die, when there's so much to discover
A little bit more than a friend

Resist it, for God's sake defend
Your grandson still needs you, Grandmother
You were always there to the end

My real mother left, you're my mother pretend
But on you I depend, there's no other
A little bit more than a friend
You were always there to the end.

Sue Simpson

WINTER GLOOM

I tread that long dark corridor
Of the deepest desolation,
As winter's army wages war.

When fog obscures the craggy tor
And clouds fly in tight formation:
I tread that long dark corridor.

A coloured world becomes no more;
Nature enters hibernation
As winter's army wages war.

When skies are ashen, sunlight poor
And the night's of day's duration:
I tread that long dark corridor.

The biting wind cuts to the core;
Leaves free-fall in wild gyration,
As winter's army wages war.

My spirit's battered, bruised and sore,
And my heart's lost dedication:
I tread that long dark corridor,
As winter's army wages war.

Wendy R Thomas

I Can't Forget

My broken heart's beyond repair.
Each day the hurt increases.
I can't forget that you're not there.

There is no comfort, none to share,
No memories appeases.
My broken heart's beyond repair.

For each foreboding thought, I swear,
My raging torrent eases.
I can't forget that you're not there.

And like a cutlass through the air,
Each painful stab releases,
My broken heart's beyond repair.

And now I only stand and stare,
My brittle pride's in pieces.
I can't forget that you're not there.

With love to spare, my cupboard's bare.
Base emptiness it squeezes.
My broken heart's beyond repair
I can't forget that you're not there.

D Haskett-Jones

THE ROSE

The rose is such a perfect flower,
What bloom has ways to speak?
A symbol that has so much power.

Given as a gift of love,
Just one small bud alone,
The rose is such a perfect flower.

Twelve red roses, says it all,
A baby's birth, a wedding ring,
The rose is such a perfect flower.

Many colours, as the rainbow holds,
Each one touches the heart,
The rose is such a perfect flower.

Picked fresh from the garden,
Dewdrops glisten like diamonds on velvet,
The rose is such a perfect flower.

No other flower speaks as loud,
Nor softens the heart, it's true.
The rose is such a perfect flower,
A symbol that has so much power.

Betty Hattersley

THE UNQUIET GRAVE

My love, it lies buried so deep, so deep.
See, here is the place where I buried it live.
I have come to the grave to weep, to weep.
How can it disturb my sleep, my sleep?
It must surely be dead. How could it survive?
My love, it lies buried so deep, so deep.
Yet tonight as the shadows creep, creep.
I feel it stir, I feel it revive.
I have come to the grave to weep, to weep.
Brown leaves of memory heap, heap
And softly cover this unquiet grave.
My love, it lies buried so deep, so deep.
If I dug there, my heart would leap
But I shall not with it connive.
I have come to the grave to weep, to weep.
But o'er this grave I watch shall keep.
I must my treacherous heart deprive.
My love it lies buried so deep, so deep.
I have come to the grave to weep, to weep.

V M Archer

JONSMAS FARE

As I sit beside the fire in the comfort of my home
and listen to the gale that blows outside
in the company of friends for I am not alone

The pig upon the spit and roasting to the bone
and with the ale the yarns are far and wide
as I sit beside the fire in the comfort of my home

In paradise we bathe and reason not to moan
the luxury of life we have to bide
in the company of friends for I am not alone

The setting of a supper enough to make you groan
and more tomorrow here we set aside
as I sit beside the fire in the comfort of my home

Tradition is a value to which we all condone
and the valour of the past we hold in pride
in the company of friends for I am not alone

The hour of the night in the time that here is shown
the culture of an evening now in slip
as I sit beside the fire in the comfort of my home
in the company of friends for I am not alone.

John M Heddle

THE BAD LANDLORD

The landlord said he'd drink to that,
When we told him we liked his beer,
We drank the toast and it was flat.

He said he was an aristocrat,
Proved it with some special beer,
The landlord said he'd drink to that.

Then what he sold us was very flat,
And the price was high and very dear,
We drank the toast and it was flat.

'It's ancient beer in that old vat,'
He said, 'No froth is just veneer,'
The landlord said he'd drink to that.

What we drank came from another vat,
'Order beer when he does appear',
We drank the toast and it was flat.

So on the landlord we won't rat,
Now he knows we revere our beer,
The landlord said he'd drink to that,
We drank the toast and it was flat.

J Lowndes-Yates

LOVE'S LAMENT

Love of my life how are you precious?
The flowers do bloom
When springtime comes

The birds migrate and then return
Just like when we first met
Love of my life how are you precious?

I deem you as my toy, my pet
The starlit sky with moon ashone
Now empty, lost, now you are gone.

My heart still lingers heavy and yet
My inner thoughts I cannot forget
Love of my life how are you precious?

Your inner beauty so far from view
Bemoaning me such solitude
I love you true.

Anguish, despair, oh sadness of heart
My emotions and world now torn apart
Love of my life how are you precious?
When springtime comes.

A E Jones

IT'S PLAIN TO SEE

In the Bible, it's plain to see,
God's Messiah, was God's leader;
Only my Christ, can set us free.

Only Christ died, instead of me,
So he must be, your true father;
In the Bible, it's plain to see.

When in that bondage, we all be,
We call out to God, our Saviour;
Only my Christ, can set us free.

Jesus was slain, upon that tree,
The Son of God, your true maker;
In the Bible, it's plain to see.

In silent tomb, beneath the lee,
He rose from Hell, our Redeemer;
Only my Christ, can set us free.

We all repent to God, like Thee,
And live with our Lord forever.
In the Bible, it's plain to see,
Only my Christ, can set us free.

F Schofield

ONE OF THE STARS BELONGS TO ME

One of the stars belongs to me
Though high in the velvety night.
As far in the Heavens as the eye can see
The star shines on in the galaxy.
Hanging like a tiny Christmas light
One of the stars belongs to me.
And it twinkles there incessantly.
'Tis sometimes gold and sometimes white
As far in the Heavens as the eye can see,
Floating on a vast blue canopy
Filling me with great delight.
A wonderful sight you must agree
Seeming to keep the world alright,
As far in the Heavens as the eye can see.
And when dawn causes the stars to flee,
I shall catch my star and hold it tight.
One of the stars belongs to me
As far in the Heavens as the eye can see.

Win Wilcock

THE NAIVETÉ OF FIRST LOVE

I swear my love would never lie.
His words are ne'er untrue.
I'd wait for him until I die.

My love for him I can't deny.
He thrills me through and through.
I swear my love would never lie.

I am the apple of his eye.
His love is ever true.
I'd wait for him until I die.

He sings to me a lullaby
With voice so dreamy too.
I swear my love would never lie.

But should he leave me I would cry.
My heart would break in two.
I'd wait for him until I die.

With hand on heart and tearful eye
As wet as morning dew.
I swear my love would never lie.
I'd wait for him until I die.

Helen Strangwige

My Soul Returns Once More

Where the sea kisses the shore.
Once my hands collected shells.
Here I seek childhood once more.

The rocks seem smaller than before.
Walking barefoot through the sand.
Where the sea kisses the shore.

High above me seagulls soar.
Like my spirit longing to be free.
Here I seek childhood once more.

Remembering imagination's open door.
Sandcastles that were full of dreams.
Where the sea kisses the shore.

Life holds so many surprises in store.
This soul needs a place to dream.
Here I seek my childhood once more.

When adult life becomes a bore.
I find comfort in memories.
Where the sea kisses the shore.
Here I seek childhood once more.

M A Challis

GRAYGREY IN NORWAY

Graygrey in Norway
Sees the midnight sun go down
On board the Black Prince

Debs is at his side
Both in nightwear pink and blue
Lovers in the night

Graygrey shows a ring
Proposes to darling Debs
Yes is the reply!

H G Griffiths

THE SCAPEGOAT

A target there to be shot at
A recipient of jealousy
Bit of a rogue - accepted
We all have frailties
Each of us fears inspection
Colleagues most of all
Hyperbole is not deception
If it is so, then -
We only deceive ourselves.

Barbara Williams

LIFE

The sun dies each night
But morning revives
So to we
Can still live our lives
Autumn sun
Still lights them.

Gladys Mary Gayler

Six Haiku

Across the hayfields
the soft wind blows tenderly
bending down the grass

Old man and grandchild
throwing snowballs in the park . . .
both young together.

Daffodils
in a vase . . .
bringing spring indoors

September morning . . .
each outline blurred and softened
in blue-grey haze.

Steely clouds parting
and Sun's pale fingers finding
diamonds in snow.

Shadow of cedar
silently crossing lawn
under April moon.

Dan Pugh

WORDS THAT BUBBLE

Poetry is like making champagne,
it needs patience and time to ferment,
don't be afraid to erase
your poor writing that calls for correction,
once satisfied, your lines maybe a verse.

Leslie Holgate

CATHEDRAL

Strong, tall, ornate pillars
made of stone,
moulded by faith through
centuries,
rooted in Durham's hills
conveying dreams.

Jean Paisley

TANKA

Last week's match programme
lies homeless at the bus stop -
seven days before
it was passed around and cherished;
now it is read by the wind.

Andrew Detheridge

THE BUDDHA

Far below the red temple,
There lies the tiled, green, Thai pagoda,
At rest, the golden Buddha.

The monsoon rain comes down,
From the black, and threatening, yellow sky,
Yet the Buddha stays dry . . .

Gordon Bannister

St Andrew's Church Prestigne

Word - church door open,
intermingling with the world
Saxon times to now.

Robert D Shooter

BIRTH - DEATH

Birth - that moment when
might be ends, what is begins,
anticipation
becomes reality and
a heartbeat becomes a life.

Death - that moment when
is ends and what was begins,
when a heartbeat stops
and a memory begins,
a second of nothingness.

Jim Sargant

DEVON

Summer is coming
Lovely the sunshine to be
Walking, swimming, outdoor fun
More meetings and more friendships
How many good summers now

Devon blooms early
Trees budding, plants showing through
Daffodils along
The roadsides untouched by crime
Where else would you find such care?

Red beaches, blue skies
Huts to lounge or shelter in
Sea to swim and play or sail
And views of such perfection
Winds can spoil a perfect time

Seagulls in plenty
Poor chance for little birds here
Some roofs attacked
Sometimes one's domestic pet
Problems but life is like that

Lovely churches here
Mixed and tolerance is good
Prominent are the old folk
So polite the young ones are
Perhaps we see the bright side.

Betty Mills

CIRCLES OF LIFE

That cotton wool sky,
I admire from way down here,
Can turn so quickly,
Bringing rain and in return,
Making life and nature whole.

E Napper

GOD'S KALEIDOSCOPE
(Haiku)

The nightingale sang
A song so sweet and tender
Then there was silence

The wind danced by
The moon so bright tonight
All up above so high

A million stars
Like diamonds in the sky
God's kaleidoscope.

June Clare

KNOWING

Teaching and learning
Wanton sponge-like brain, soaking
Knowledge and knowing.

Writing and describing
Know what people feel and gain
Taken from their life.

Sadness and losing
From life we have to learn all
Through hardships, and pain.

Susan Carole Roberts

the curtains.

WRITTEN IN EARLY OCTOBER

You held white bouquets
for a while - but now offer
berries for birds.
Pale - to dark transformation
glimpsed under October skies.

So tiny, starry -
flowers caught in memory.
Left - only black dots
Yet how they glitter, glisten
for all who are seeking them.

Two wines for mankind -
elderflower or berry -
a banquet for birds -
thanks be to you, Elder Tree
for this fruit of ebony.

C M Creedon

MISTY MOORS

Purple moors
colourful and delicate
clusters of bell flowers
treasures of cotton
grass, here to stay.

Alan Hattersley

EXPRESSIONS OF WORDS

Up and down,
Round and round,
Without even knowing,
From my mind,
These words are flowing
Writing poems; my heart
is flowing.

Anon

PEACE

In the ancient church
Musty, damp, autumnal walls
Passive and silent.

Wendy Dedicott

SEPTEMBER RAIN

And loving, hurting,
August, descended into
A falsehood of love:

Why would this darkness
Of spirit surround me now,
In September rain?

Edmund Saint George Mooney

A SET OF HAIKU

September brambles -
Rain creates berries' juice -
Sunshine their sweetness.

Red and green knots swell
And ripen through purple, till
They're teacher's-ink black.

On balmy June nights
Roses haul fragrance around
Frames of pergolas.

Gillian Fisher

I SEE THE LIGHT

Though darkness holds us -
I see the morning sunrise
Rising in the sky.

Marcus Tyler